The HR Genie

Jeremy Francis

Amended version, with articles
.

ACKNOWLEDGEMENTS

Special thanks to Aileen Kelley, for invaluable feedback and advice. Also to Robert Mowser, for the wonderful illustrations.

CONTENTS

Author's Note

It took me exactly one month to start, and finish this book. And to make things more interesting, I typed the entire thing on my mobile phone. That was great, because, whenever I was stuck in a line at the bank, or waiting to pick up the kids from school, I'd just take out my phone and start typing away.

It didn't take long to type, but the story of Raj has been long in coming. Basically, the book looks at starting a Performance Management System from scratch, and draws on my experience of doing this for a few of my consulting clients. It is by no means a perfect plan, nor will you be able to implement a full system by the time you get through it. But, you will get a sense for what the major issues are, and with some work (on your part), you will be well on your way to creating something workable.

Performance Management is a very complex topic. And a lot of companies get it wrong. The main problem is that it's often treated as a separate, standalone aspect of HR, and it really is not.

So have a read and see if it helps.

Or, you can always summon Raj…

The material in this book is for educational purposes only. This book is sold with the understanding that neither the author nor the publisher assumes any liability for any errors or omission, or how this book or its contents are used or interpreted, or any consequences resulting directly or indirectly from the use of this book. For legal advice or any other, please consult your personal lawyer or the appropriate professional.

Illustrations by Robert Mowser.

Throughout this book, the Cambria type font was used for headlines, and text was set using Times New Roman font.

1 Bad News Monday

Tracy did not want to get up that morning. The alarm clock was the first casualty, as she knocked it to the floor. She was certain that it would not be the last. Her performance appraisal awaited her this morning. 8:30 on a Monday morning. It was not going to go well. Ms. Rogers, the HR Director, would ensure that it did not.

Ms. Rogers was one of the most unfriendly persons Tracy had ever met, and she always wondered how she had managed to become HR Director with that attitude. Tracy had been tasked with implementing a Performance Management System, and it had gone horribly wrong. There were missed deadlines. Added to this, were the unsupportive supervisors and managers. And, to top it off, little guidance from senior management like Ms. Rogers.

Tracy's partner on the project, Rodney, would be in the same predicament had it not been for his ability to charm a stone. Tracy, on the other hand, hated to deal with executives. They made her uncomfortable. Maybe it was because she thought that they were all arrogant. Most executives she had met were.

She climbed out of bed, sidestepped the pieces of the alarm clock on the floor, dressed and got into her car in record time. She knew by now not to keep that woman waiting. Never a minute early or late, Ms. Rogers always magically appeared on time and expected everyone else to do the same.

As Tracy made the familiar journey to the office, she reflected on just how she had gotten into this mess. She was twenty-two and had graduated top of her class with a first degree in Human Resource Management from a local university. She enrolled in and was selected to be a part of the Graduate Training Program at Capital Investments Inc., a financial services company that was well established in the country and the region.

This is where she currently works.

The company has seven affiliates in other territories. In the home country, it employs about 400 employees across five branches. Tracy and most of the other graduates work at the head office which is also the regional headquarters. All major decisions are made here, and it contains most of the executive offices which makes it a great place to be if you want to get noticed. But that could be a double-edged sword as Tracy had begun to realize.

She, along with some of the other top graduates from her class, had been quickly snapped up by the recruiter and, after a lengthy interview and induction process, she had started in the HR department six months ago.

Rodney, with whom she was good friends from university days, had also gone through the same process. The first few months were great. They had many opportunities to learn from the different departments, participated in team builders and even completed a few training courses.

The fun ended when they met Ms. Rogers. She was not impressed with their degrees or, according to her, their 'pitiful work ethic'. She had assigned the graduate trainees a series of projects based on their study areas, and Tracy and Rodney were initially happy with their project to *'Develop a new Performance Management System procedure for the company'*.

It seemed simple enough. This was an area of particular interest to Tracy, and she loved doing research. The duration of their internship was only one year, and the outcome of this project would determine whether they would be offered permanent positions.

Tracy could see a future for herself at the company and was hoping to stay on after the end of her internship period. Now she was not so sure.

By now, Tracey and Rodney were halfway through their internship, and the project was going horribly wrong - just in time for their mid-year review with Ms. Rogers.

"Dude, this will not go well."

Rodney was in the habit of calling all his peers 'dude', regardless of gender. Tracy had had six months to get used to it. She still was not.

That was yesterday. As she pulled into the parking lot with about ten minutes to spare, she had a real sense of foreboding. The fact that it was overcast was not helpful.

She had just enough time to put her things at her desk before it was time to make her way to the review meeting. Rodney looked at her solemnly and bowed his head in prayer. His turn would come after.

2 The Review

Ms. Rogers' assistant ushered Tracy into the office. She sensed her unease and tried to make her feel comfortable. It didn't work.

"Don't worry," she said, "she is always tough on the ones she likes."

She must love me, Tracy thought.

She remembered her first interaction with Ms. Rogers. The group of trainees had just finished a meeting with Brian, the CEO. He was a very amiable man who insisted that they call him by his first name. He was more of a motivational speaker than an executive, and he had them all shouting and screaming company slogans by the time he was finished. Tracy blames him for allowing her guard to be let down. After the great pep talk, they were offered up to the dragon.

"Most of you will not be here at the end of the year," she began. "We strive for excellence and most of you will not meet our standards."

The chill in the room was real.

She went on to talk about the importance of the HR Department and the work that was going on.

"We are in the process of revamping our entire Performance Management System, and some of you may have the privilege of working on this project."

At the time, Tracy was excited about that, but now not so much.

"Your degrees may have gotten you here, but your level of competence will determine whether you will stay."

Tracy did not feel at all competent in that moment.

Soon after this meeting the graduates were split into project teams. There were four HR trainees. Two were selected for a compensation project, while Tracy and Rodney got the nod to revamp the Performance Management System.

"We're going to ace this," she had said at the time. "We both did really well on our class project on this topic."

Indeed they had. Tracy's team got one of the highest scores that year for their Performance Management project and she was especially proud since she had done most of the work. She hated group projects but decided to do whatever was necessary to maintain her A average. Rodney was the only other person in the group to pull his weight.

"Yeah, but dude, this is no class project." Rodney was right.

The project seemed simple enough. They had to review the current Performance Management System of the company, come up with specific recommendations to improve it and run a pilot of the new system in the Records Department. Tracy did not know this at the time, but the Records Department was known to be difficult because the manager, Mr. Gregg, was famous for his perfectionist behavior. This was fine for the Head of the department responsible for maintaining accurate records of the company's clients and transactions. But his exceptional attention to detail drove those who had to work with him crazy.

"Tracy, I noticed that your last document sent for my review had fifteen spelling errors and nine grammatical inconsistencies," he had told her once. "You're going to want to fix that before I approve it."

It had taken three more attempts and several softly spoken expletives before he gave it the go ahead.

That was only part of the problem she had had with the project. Every time a change was made there was a lengthy process of approval and, as a result, the project timeline was in disarray.

Then there were the department supervisors. There were thirty-five employees in the Records Department and five supervisors, each one more quarrelsome than the last. They didn't like the format of the new appraisal form. They didn't like the metrics. They complained that it was more work for them. She had almost given up.

"Don't worry, I will sort them out," Rodney had told her.

She was happy that he was her partner because, more often than not, he was able to charm them into going along with the plan but only after some serious convincing.

Their new Performance Management System looked good on paper. It tied in nicely with the compensation and training plans and even had a link to management and executive succession. The redesigned employee appraisal form was twice as long as the old one, but it covered a lot more areas that their research showed were key to the industry they operated in.

The competencies were taken from the latest management books and periodicals, so she was sure that they were on the right track. Some of the others were found using Google. In the end, Tracy and Rodney had to stop the project once Ms. Rogers got involved. Unfortunately for them, this could also mean the end of their career with the firm.

3 The Details

Ms. Rogers sat at one end of the long conference table, and Tracy sat at the other. She was flipping through some papers on the desk. Tracy tried to keep her heart rate down. After about two minutes of this torture, Ms. Rogers spoke.

"Enjoying your time with us?" she asked, without looking up from the papers on the desk.

Tracy was just able to mumble something that sounded like a yes.

"Well, based on the way this project went, I would have thought that HR is probably not the best career choice."

Tracy was determined not to lose her composure. Not today.

She asked Tracy to give her a synopsis of the project and where she thought things went wrong.

Tracy was prepared for this. She indicated that even though she had enjoyed working with the Records Department – strictly speaking this was true – she thought that their structure made it too difficult for such a system to work effectively.

"So, you're basically saying that you were not able to get them to follow your lead."

"No, I'm saying that the structure of the department makes performance difficult to measure." Tracy's blood pressure was rising.

"Well dear, that is why they were chosen. It makes little sense to pilot a new system where results are easy to come by. There could be a bigger crash when it is rolled out across the entire company, so it's always best to treat with the most difficult first."

Tracy could not argue against this logic, but she still felt strongly that Records was a bad choice. She was unable to convince Ms. Rogers.

"Still, choice of department was not your main problem. Your methodology and process were horrendous," she said, while poking a finger at what Tracy realized was one of her reports.

"We adhered to some of the latest findings used by international companies..." she began, only to be cut off by the HR Director.

"...but it had very little bearing on our reality here or the complexities of this organization."

Tracy remembered having a similar argument with one of her lecturers about a paper she had done as part of her studies. She had walked out of his office in a huff back then. Unfortunately, she could not try that this time, not without having to walk straight out of the building and into her car never to return.

Ms. Rogers went on to tear her project apart from the metrics that were used to the appraisal form.

"As it stands, the managers hate to fill out these forms," she mused, "and your solution is to make it twice as long?"

Rodney had expressed the same doubts, but she had been adamant that it was the only way to cover all the competencies.

"And where did these competency definitions come from?"

Tracy decided that it was not a good idea to mention Google.

She had to sit there for another half hour as Ms. Rogers tore into her work. She was numb, exhausted and depressed. But, thankfully, she was able to keep a straight face.

Ms. Rogers stated that the company needed the Performance Management System to do three things:

- Identify key talent in the organization

- Increase the competence base of all employees

- Ensure that there are sufficient candidates for upward and lateral movement

"I cannot do these things with this," she said, as she closed the file with a deep sigh.

Tracy said nothing. There wasn't anything to say. She had tuned out most of what was said, but she knew that the project had failed.

Her first clue was the push back from the supervisors. Then there was the difficulty in quantifying the results. But she was convinced that with a little more time and a more willing test department, she would have gotten it right. Not according to Ms. Rogers.

"Be that as it may, you have a chance to redeem it."

Tracy was listening again.

"I expect a new draft of the Performance Management System in two weeks, complete with a roll-out plan. And you have to do the roll-out in Records."

Ms. Rogers may as well have told her to resign.

4 The Briefcase

It was Friday evening and Tracy was working late. It was already 8:00pm, and she was still not sure when she would be leaving. Her deadline was looming and much remained undone. Ms. Rogers had removed Rodney from the project and put him on the compensation team. Tracy had not spoken to him since.

She wasn't really upset with him but was sure that his silver tongue had gotten him out of trouble as it usually did.

Tracy was in the old storeroom looking through some old HR files as part of her research.

Ms. Rogers had suggested that she look through these files to get some background information on how HR was done and how the company had developed in the early years. Even though the company was fully computerized, these old files were not in the system.

Tracy would have preferred to skip this assignment, but she had learned early on that a suggestion from Ms. Rogers was actually a directive.

She was now looking through training records and old employees files to see how performance reviews were done in the past. The Records Department was responsible for these old files and had done a great job of organizing them. The files she wanted were easy enough to find, but the volume meant she that would be here for a while.

Despite herself, she actually started enjoying going through the files and learning about the company's history.

She was seeing some interesting trends so far. There seemed to have been no correlation between job performance and career path in many of the old employee files she looked at, and different departments had different competencies, sometimes for the same job function. More importantly, some of these persons were still with the company.

Some positions had no job description at all. At least the current system had sorted that out, and appraisals were pretty much standardized across the company. But the link to career planning and succession planning was tenuous at best.

For Tracy, the main difficulty was in creating a transparent system that was able to accurately assess an employee's performance thereby allowing for appropriate planning to take place. There was too much room for subjectivity.

At the very least, there was enough information to put together a detailed history of the company, but that would have to be a project for another time – granted that she was still here, of course.

As she was about to replace some files into the ancient filing cabinet, a few that were precariously perched on top slid off and fell behind.

When she tried to push it forward to retrieve the fallen files, the entire cabinet fell over with a loud crash.

Tracy was willing to attribute this to the improvement in her upper body strength from being in the gym five days a week, but also had to admit to the fact that the cabinet appeared to be top-heavy.

While cursing her luck and bending to pick up the papers strewn across the floor, she noticed what appeared to be an old suitcase wedged in the bottom drawer.

Her eyes were drawn to it. She had never seen a briefcase like it before, and she had seen many a briefcase. It seemed pretty old but wasn't falling apart. In fact, were it not for the dust and a few wear and tear marks, it looked usable.

"Looks as ancient as Ms. Rogers!" she exclaimed as she lifted it out of the drawer.

There was a strange inscription written on one side, etched into the leather, but the dust made it difficult to read. The weight suggested that there was something inside, and curiosity got the better of her.

She carried it to the table in the centre of the room and laid it flat. The writing was still unintelligible. The more she looked at it, the greater her desire to get it opened became.

"Maybe I'll find my Performance Management System in here," she joked as she ran her fingers gently over the inscription.

She started to dust away the residue from the surface with her hands when something very strange happened.

The briefcase started vibrating, and the table began to shake. Smoke started pouring out of the sides. In a state of panic, Tracy flung the briefcase to the corner of the room and ran towards the door. As she scampered to the exit, the door slammed shut, and the room filled with smoke. Before long, she passed out.

5 The Visitor

When Tracy eventually came to, she was laying on the sofa that lined one wall of the storeroom. The mess of papers had been cleared up, and the cabinet was back in position. Everything seemed to be in order – everything except for the large man in a crumpled business suit that was sitting across from her at the table.

It was times like these that made Tracy wish that she had completed the Jiu-Jitsu classes at the gym.

"W...who are you?" she stammered, trying to hide the fear and uncertainty in her voice.

The strange round man looked up from the papers he was studying on the desk.

He seemed old but also young at the same time. He had one of those faces from which you couldn't really tell how old the person was. And his skin was brown. The kind of brown that paper turned in a really old book.

But his eyes were his main feature. They were large and dark, and despite herself, Tracy felt calm and safe. She did not feel threatened which was outstanding considering that she was in the basement of a building with a strange man whom she had never seen before.

"Who am I?" he asked, looking surprised. "It depends on who you ask really, but the more important question is why?"

"Why...what?"

Tracy was already calculating how quickly she could get to the door.

"Oh, the door is open Tracy. You are not being held against your will and you can leave at any time. As to the question of who I am, seeing that you summoned me, I thought that you already knew."

She vaguely remembered what had happened with the suitcase and, for some reason, she thought of genies from Arabic tales.

"Well, I've been called that before," the round man chuckled, "and although not the most flattering, it's certainly not the worst description I've heard. If you are comfortable with that, then yes, I am a genie and, in keeping with the stories, I am here to give you three wishes, or in this case, free consulting advice. This is the why."

Tracy was beginning to think that this was one of Rodney's pranks. There was probably a hidden camera somewhere. This entire episode would most likely be making the rounds on social media tomorrow.

"Oh no, Rodney has nothing to do with this. He is at dinner with friends where you would be too if you didn't have this problem."

Rodney did invite her to go out that evening but she had declined, partly because of this research and also because she was still upset with him. She knew how to hold a grudge. But this strange man could not know that. He seemed to be reading her mind.

"Wait, hang on. How do you know my name and about..."

"Your disastrous project? Yes, I know about it. Be careful, you can only ask me three questions related to HR and your project. Choose them wisely."

Tracy was dumbstruck. If she were to follow the illogical argument, this man was a genie who lived in the suitcase and she had let him out. Now he was offering her three wishes, or consulting advice as he put it, to help get the performance management project back on track.

She decided that she was dreaming. Perhaps she was actually in bed right now, sleeping off the effects of an extra alcoholic beverage or two. If only her recollection of opening the suitcase and being confronted with this strange scene was not so vivid.

"I like your thought process. It's not that far off," the strange man said. "I am here to help you with this project and nothing more.

You are free to ask for help, and you are free to ignore this opportunity. You are free."

He placed the briefcase on the table.

"What…what is your name? Can you at least tell me that?"

She hoped that this would not count as one of her wishes.

"My name? I have been called many things. Some of the names are too long for your comprehension. You can call me Raj. Yes, that should be fine."

Raj. She couldn't make this up even if she wanted to.

"I know this is a lot to take in, so I will leave you for now. But I must make you aware of the rules."

Of course, Tracy thought, *why could I not just imagine something simple?*

"The first rule is that you must tell no one about me. This is non-negotiable. Secondly, for the duration of my assistance, you must keep this briefcase with you at all times – it is our link. Finally, your questions must be very specific. Choose them carefully or my ability to assist you will be limited."

This seemed simple enough, if she decided to buy into this nonsense.

I know it is a lot to take in, so go, have a rest." Raj said in an understanding tone. "Take the briefcase with you and, when you are ready, do what you did the first time to summon me."

With that he was gone, and Tracy was alone. She couldn't say definitively that he had disappeared. She just knew that he wasn't there anymore. All that remained was the briefcase.

As she headed out of the building with the case under her arm, she reflected on the evening's events. She felt she must be going crazy. At least she might be able to get the help she needed to get the project done. There was only one way to find out.

6 The First Question

Tracy had a very strange weekend indeed. Every time she fell asleep, she believed that when she woke up the suitcase would be gone and that Friday's events would turn out to have just been a dream.

But every time she awoke the briefcase was still there. So she slept a lot to make it go away. It did not. The briefcase itself seemed to be changing too. As the weekend progressed and her doubts grew stronger, it started looking older and more worn.

"By the time I go to work on Monday morning, it will have turned to dust," she mused.

She was not really sure what to make of all this.

On Monday morning she had a new problem – the briefcase did not match with any of her work suits.

At the very least, if I have to walk around with this ugly thing, I might as well try to look good doing it.

She flung it across the bed and two additional scars appeared on the surface. It was as if she had hurt the briefcase's feelings and it reflected this in physical damage.

She decided to play nice from then on, lest she be mistaken for an old bag lady as she made her way to the office with it on her arm.

She decided to go in early in an attempt to escape most of the prying eyes. The security guard gave her a curious look when he saw the briefcase but said nothing.

She made her way quickly to her cubicle and put it under her desk. She tried to plan her day. Together with some of the other trainees in Compensation and Training, she had several meetings with the manager and supervisors of the Records Department. She was the only one working on her project, but she had to work closely with the others to get it done. It was one of the things she was doing differently from the last time.

She had a week left until her deadline and a mountain of work still to do.

Soon the HR Department began filling up. She tried to stay out of the way and distanced herself from the weekend updates.

Oh Tracy, what did you do this weekend? She mockingly asked herself. *Oh, I spent it with a strange man that lives in a briefcase.*

She was sure that wouldn't go down well.

Soon Rodney came in. She tried to look busy at her desk. He sat right next to her, so there was no escaping him.

"Hey, we were looking out for you on Friday and Satur...what the hell is that?" he exclaimed as he noticed the old, dusty bag at her feet.

"That, ummm...I brought up some old files from the storeroom and it made sense just to take it at the time."

She hoped that it would not lead to more questions. The briefcase seemed to have aged fifty years since she got in that morning.

"Well, keep that away from me. It looks like it fought with a rat and lost." She could not disagree.

When he tried to find out how the project was going, she steered him away from the topic. It wasn't something she wanted to discuss with him; plus there were the rules to consider – she could not tell anyone about what happened.

She also could not believe that she was falling for it.

Her meetings were difficult enough without having to drag the ancient briefcase along with her.

The looks she got went from mild amusement to terror and it was hard trying to keep a straight face. If this ended up being a cruel joke, there would be hell to pay. She had lost all the style points that were carefully accumulated over the past few months in one morning.

The meetings tested her patience. The supervisors were still having issues with the metrics she had come up with and could not agree on the definitions or the points system. Mr. Gregg was not helpful either.

"Young lady, you are giving them more work to do," he had told her. "That significantly reduces the likelihood that they will do it."

She wanted to seriously reduce the likelihood of having a nervous breakdown by the end of the week.

By the close of business that day, Tracy was drained. But she had to find out if there was any merit to this whole adventure with the briefcase. She and the bag both looked exhausted, and as her coworkers left she made her way to the storeroom.

Once there, she quickly glanced around to see if she was alone and to make sure that there were no hidden cameras. She still wasn't convinced that this was not part of a very elaborate ploy. She would not put it past Rodney. She could imagine him putting a video of her up on the big screen in the conference room just before the weekly meeting with all trainees.

She put the briefcase on the table. It was in a very dilapidated state by now. It looked as sad as she felt.

"Well, I might as well get over it," she said to herself. "Moment of truth."

She brushed her hand gently over the inscription on the front panel, but nothing happened. She did it again.

Still nothing.

Figures.

She just might have to make that appointment to see the Employee Assistance Program psychiatrist after all.

"No need to call twice," a voice behind her said. "One time is enough."

With her heart in her mouth, Tracy spun around, and there was Raj, standing next to a whiteboard.

"How did you...?"

"One of my many powers" he chuckled. "Come, we have little time and much to discuss."

Her mind was racing. She remembered the third rule about being specific, but she had so many questions it was difficult to pick one. Half of them had nothing to do with her project but were instead about Raj.

He sensed her confusion.

"Don't worry, all your concerns will be addressed, but first let us focus on the task at hand. For your first question, I may be a little lax, since you are new to all this. But as a hint, start with what is troubling you most."

She thought about this. She was getting nowhere fast with the project and could not understand why.

"Why is measuring performance so difficult?"

The words flew out of her mouth before she had time to think about it.

Raj seemed pleased.

"Ah, excellent way to start. Allow me to begin our first consultation."

He waved his hand over the whiteboard, and words appeared.

"What is Performance Management?"

Tracy thought that she would be the one to ask the questions.

"Humor me and tell me what you think it is."

She thought for a minute. Then she delivered a Masters worthy definition compiled from a combination of journal articles and textbooks. Halfway through, Raj pretended to fall asleep.

Everyone was making fun of her today.

"Oh, I'm sorry, are you finished?" Raj let out a loud yawn.

"The first thing you will learn is that if you have to memorize it, it's probably not worth remembering.

In one sentence, he had just devalued her entire academic career.

"By that I mean, if it does not come to your mind naturally it will be hard to remember and even harder to implement."

He waved his hand at the whiteboard and the words disappeared.

"The best way to explain it is to show you."

With that, Raj disappeared. And so did she, Tracy soon realized.

7 The Value Proposition

They were now in a room similar to the one they had just left. In the centre, three people were sitting at a table with what appeared to be a set of toy building blocks. All of them were blindfolded and they were trying to build a tower as high as they possibly could.

This meant that as soon as the tower reached a decent height one of them would accidentally knock it over, and they would have to start again. What made it even worse was that some of the blocks fell off the table and, since they could not see where the blocks had fallen, they were left with fewer blocks each time.

"At some point, all organizations have this problem," Raj began as he and Tracy sat behind the group. "They try to make more with less. The problem is that some organizations handicap their employees by not making the vision or direction of the organisation clear to them."

Just at that moment, the tower fell again, and the builders dutifully started over with even fewer blocks.

"Eventually, a stalemate is reached and the employees cannot deliver what the employer wants. The value proposition fails."

This all felt strangely familiar to Tracy. It was akin to working on this project with no clear end game. She knew what the outcome had to be but was unclear of the direction to go or what was expected.

"So, they keep working, and they keep failing. It becomes normal. Bad performance becomes normal. Bad service becomes normal. Employees deliver it, customers expect it, and the cycle continues."

They moved over to a second table.

Three people were here as well, but no one was blindfolded this time. They were actually doing quite well, and the tower was going up at a very fast pace. Suddenly, one of the builders purposefully knocked over the blocks. This led to a heated argument. Hair was pulled. Expletives were used. It was a messy situation.

"At other times, the goal is clear. Performance is high and the product is good. Then someone with a competing interest sabotages the process because his or her goals are undermined by the success of others. Again, the value proposition fails."

This too made sense to Tracy. She had participated in many group projects where one or two members did their best to make life difficult for the others. Why? It was usually when they did not get their way.

They went over to a third group. Just like the second, they were working like a well-oiled machine. Midway through their tower construction, another person entered the fray. She stopped them and said a few words- after which they dismantled the tower. The new participant then took away some of the blocks.

The group started building again, but this time they came up with ingenious ways to build the tower to the same height using the few blocks they remained with.

"Every now and again the value proposition is achieved. The vision is clear. When disruption happens, it is anticipated, and the team reacts accordingly. Product quality is maintained. Customer satisfaction is not compromised. Perfection."

As he said that, Raj let out a sigh of satisfaction. Tracy felt good too.

"So Tracy, which company do you think has a Performance Management System?" Raj asked, as he waved his hand and they reappeared in the storeroom.

"That's easy, the third one," she said, enjoying the sensation of moving through space.

"In that case you are wrong." Raj said. "They all have a system in place but only one of them works."

This did not make sense to Tracy.

"But it's obvious that the first two..."

"...don't have one because they were failing at their job? Trust me when I say that all companies have a Performance Management System whether they intended it or not."

He directed her back to the first question he asked.

"Simply put, Performance Management Systems are a set of conditions that seek to reward certain behaviors and discourage others – like classical conditioning."

She did not see how this related to the first two scenarios.

"It's all about goal directed behavior," he went on, "since people require motivation to get things done and if the organization does not provide it, people will invent forms of motivation."

He went on to explain that systems of managing performance exist whether or not a company has a formal system.

"In the first scenario, those folks could have been motivated simply by the joy of working blindfolded and knocking over the blocks or by having no real purpose other than playing with blocks. The second group could have been motivated by their own self-interest or by a desire to ensure that no one else succeeded. The third group was motivated by something else – a value proposition."

Tracy understood that all the groups were motivated, albeit by different things. But she had always believed that motivation led to a positive result.

"Motivation does not always lead to a positive result." Raj chimed in, reading her mind.

"It all boils down to the ability to motivate people to do something we want and discourage them from doing something we would prefer they not do. The way this is done isn't always to the benefit of all," he said as he moved towards the whiteboard again.

"In an organizational setting, there are a number of tools at our disposal to motivate employees with the aim of getting them to do better – compensation and benefits, training and development, promotion and more. A Performance Management System is just an integrated way of using these tools to get the best out of people at work."

Tracy was beginning to feel like a hamster in a spinning wheel.

"What gets done is what gets rewarded. If the goal is not clear, there will be no proper way to improve performance."

"So my dear, now you have to find the value proposition, not only for your project but for the Performance Management System that you were asked to build. And don't call on me until you know what it is."

With those parting words, Tracy was alone again.

8 A New Perspective

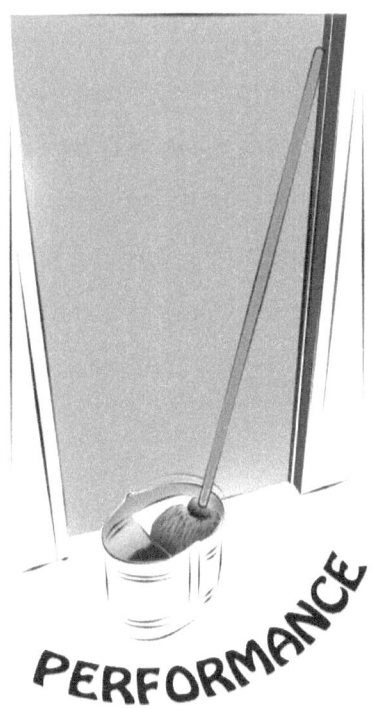

PERFORMANCE

Tracy was still in shock about being left on her own, just when she had the most questions. She wanted to summon Raj back but knew that she had a lot more than two questions on her mind.

She thought about what she had just experienced. To her, it seemed that it should be clear to employees exactly what the purpose of their work is since they expected to be properly compensated for it. She also knew that this was rarely the case. Most employers feel that employees are not generally working as hard as they should be, and employees generally feel that employers are not compensating them enough for the work that they are doing not to mention the extra work that they always believed they did.

This was one of the primary reasons why, in her opinion, Performance Management Systems were developed. Such a system serves as a way of clarifying goals and rewarding their achievement. It also identifies gaps and promotes corrective action in the form of training or eventual separation.

But is there more to it?

It seemed that people only do things for a reason and, if the reason is not clear, they make up one to justify their effort. The implication of this is that, if a clear basis for work is not provided, chances are that employees would make up their own reasons which might be in conflict with what management wants.

But is it not clear to everyone what the reason or the purpose behind their work is?

She thought about a simple task like cleaning the floor. How much more was there to it besides taking a mop and applying it to the floor? There is no science to that. Yet, she had to admit that some of the cleaning personnel at the firm did a poor job of even this simple task. Are they going to have measurable performance targets too? Would they have to get an appraisal form done and a score that ranks their performance? The idea seemed silly to her. Sometimes a reprimand was enough to get it sorted, at least for a couple of weeks.

She thought about the value proposition. It seemed to her that this was the reason for work. The goal. The vision. She worked for a financial services company. Is it not obvious that the value proposition is to sell financial products at a profit?

Tracy thought about that some more. This was not her value proposition. Neither was it the value proposition of the Records Department. She didn't sell financial products and, if she did, she would be horrible at it.

Her job and that of the Records Department was to support those who did sell financial products. The Records Department did this by ensuring that all relevant documentation was stored properly and was easily accessible when needed. Her role was to...*what was her role exactly?*

She worked in HR performing tasks in a number of HR functions but how did these functions specifically add value to the sale of financial products?

She was starting to get a headache. She knew in general terms that her work contributed to the development of the company, or so she would like to believe. Still, the more she thought about it the more unclear she was about how her specific job and tasks related to the bigger picture of selling financial products.

I guess that in helping to recruit the right people and by rewarding them properly, HR supports the business in a direct way, she mused, *but if I were to try and measure the effectiveness of HR at doing this in a specific way, can I?*

She had no answers.

She got the feeling that this was what Raj meant by the value proposition. Maybe the first step was to find out what each department specifically did to support the overall work of the company and find a way to use the Performance Management System to measure their effectiveness at doing it. This sounded simple enough.

Then she thought of something.

Isn't the value proposition of each department based on something, like the vision and mission of the company itself?

She tried to remember the company's vision and mission. She passed them every morning at the front desk where they resided in a large picture frame. She could not remember the words. This was not surprising. She was sure it was the same for most employees. They were all primarily concerned with the work on their desks and meeting the targets set by their managers. But were those targets in line with the overall vision and mission of the company?

She remembered her last vacation internship. It was with a company in the energy sector and ended up being a paid holiday. The interns did not have much to do other than filing and helping to proofread documents and presentations. Occasionally, they went on a training course. She didn't complain because the previous semester had been difficult, and she had not been in the mood for hard work. But she remembered being extremely bored. To counter it, she spent most of her ample free time on social media.

What was the value proposition in this case? For the company, it was probably to give students an opportunity to get an income and some work experience, and maybe it was also a chance for the company to identify talent for hire in the future. For the interns, it was an opportunity to be away from home, make an income and possibly line up a job after graduation.

The actual experience, however, left a lot to be desired. The supervisors and managers had little interest in the process beyond making the interns extensions of the office furniture and equipment. As a result, the interns did not learn much from the experience. The value proposition was lost. The stated and the eventual outcomes were different.

Sometimes the best intentions are never realized, and lofty goals are never met, but why?

She knew where she could get the answers.

The next day Tracy went to see Mr. Gregg, the manager of the Records Department. She asked him about the vision and mission of his department.

"Oh, we are starting to ask questions now instead of giving the answers?

Tracy blushed since she knew that, in all of their meetings, she had never really been keen to understand the work of the department but was focused on getting them to conform to her plan.

"In order for this project to work, I realize that I need to better understand how the department functions and the reasoning behind how things are done. Only then will I be able to build a system to assess its effectiveness," she conceded.

For the next half hour, Mr. Gregg went through with her, in detail, the structure of the department and the functions of all the staff. He even showed her a copy of his operational plan which broke down key elements of the company's strategic plan for his department.

"Every year, when the strategic plan is finalized, we spend a lot of time translating it into objectives for the department," he explained. "We have to get these objectives approved, along with budgets, and then we roll it out to the entire staff."

This seemed to be where the value proposition came from.

"The problem with your Performance Management System, Tracy, is that it never really took into consideration this aspect of our work. All you focused on were personality quirks and a bunch of loaded statements that did not reflect much of what we did here."

Normally, she would have been offended by this description of her metrics and appraisal format, but she could see that it was true.

"I understand that you have your own objectives to measure, but I always thought that the system was supposed to manage our performance, not the perception by HR of what our performance should be," Mr. Gregg continued.

His words stung, but he was right. Over the course of the last few weeks, Tracy had been trying to introduce a set of measures that she had collected from a series of different sources. Her attempt to implement them had met with much resistance.

At that moment, she recognized a problem.

"How, then, do we standardize a system if we leave it up to each department to define what is to be measured. Where is the consistency in that?"

"Hey, that is what you guys in HR get paid the big bucks to find out," he joked. "All I know is that if your system is not specific to the work that we do, it will always be a struggle to implement it. If the system is too generic, it will never measure what you want it to, and it will be a big waste of time."

Tracy felt it was time to see Raj again.

9 The Second Question

Something strange was happening to the briefcase. Since her last encounter with Raj and her meeting with Mr. Gregg the day after, it seemed to have repaired itself. It no longer looked like something she had dragged out of the gutter and was starting to look normal enough to go unnoticed. She assumed that it was reflecting her growing optimism as she made progress and for this she was grateful.

She was ready to meet with Raj again but first she requested a consult with Ms. Rogers on the strategic planning process. Her face did not show it but Ms. Rogers was pleased.

"This process is integral to your project, as it should inform the management of staff performance," she said as she gave Tracy a document. "This is the full version of our five year strategic plan. We are currently in year three. It may be helpful."

Tracy had seen some of the company's strategic planning documents before, but this was the full plan and was considered highly confidential. The look on Ms. Rogers' face told her that she was being entrusted with an important document and that she needed to be careful with it.

She also seemed uncommonly interested in the briefcase but said nothing about it.

Later that evening, Tracy headed for the storeroom, but one of the office cleaners was in there. After a few impatient moments spent waiting for the cleaner to finish, she entered and closed the door. She rubbed the inscription on the bag, and there was Raj, sitting next to her.

"I trust that you did your homework?" he asked while flipping through a copy of what looked like the document Ms. Rogers gave to her. She didn't bother to ask how he got it.

"Yes, and I've realized that the value proposition *is the guiding principle that governs the work of an organization. It is the statement that defines what we do and how we should do it.*"

Some might call it the strategic plan, but she realized that it was a bit more than that. It was the element that defined specifically what work is done and how. Once this is properly defined, it can be measured by a Performance Management System.

"Very good!" Raj exclaimed. "I could not have put it better myself. Care to give me an example?"

She thought about the cleaning lady who had just left the room.

"Well, the cleaning lady's job is to clean," she started, "but in order for it to be done properly or to the required standard there has to be some guidelines like what cleaning products to use, when to clean and how often. And it should be inspected for quality control."

Raj's smile was getting wider. She was encouraged.

"So, the value proposition is not only that the room needs to be cleaned, but there has to be guidance on the method or process by which it is to be done in order that it can be checked to ensure that the standard is met."

"Head to the top of the class!" Raj shouted.

Tracy was really was pleased with herself.

"But that is just the beginning. Do you have another question for me?"

She had thought carefully about this one. There were many questions swimming around in her head, but she figured that choosing the right one would result in answers to several others. Finally, she blurted out,

"How do you measure actual performance?"

"Ah, the million dollar question," Raj said as he walked over to the whiteboard that was not there a minute ago. He was writing.

"Well, we have to examine this question first."

What is Performance?

"What does it mean to say that someone has performed or not?"

Tracy thought for a minute.

"Well, I can think of it on a couple levels," she responded.

"In the case of the cleaner, a task is assigned and she is asked to perform an action or series of actions that lead to a particular result. In order to know if the task was performed there would need to be a particular outcome, something visible to indicate that it was done."

Raj was writing on the whiteboard again.

"On the other hand, the cleaner could just be told to clean the floor with no other instructions or guidelines. This would mean that she would have to use her own standards which may not always be in line with what her supervisor wants. This could lead to poor performance and conflict."

She looked at the whiteboard. Raj had written down the following equation:

$$\textbf{\textit{Direction}} \times \textbf{\textit{Motivation}} = \textbf{\textit{Reward}}$$

"Then there is the issue of motivation," Raj added. "Humans are goal-directed creatures. If they lack purpose, they will lack motivation. If the organization does not provide this purpose, chances are that motivation will be either absent or misdirected."

It is because of this the value proposition is so important, Raj explained. Without the context that it provides, it is difficult to manage performance and the underlying motivation which is required to achieve it.

He told her that some people call this employee engagement.

"In cases where the employee is demotivated," he explained, "it will be difficult to implement a Performance Management System. Since there is no agreement on what the outcome should look like, the system will not be as effective. Employees will work based on their own motivations. Managers will complain. And everyone will hate to fill out appraisal forms."

Tracy knew this to be true. Everyone hated appraisal forms. Most of the forms she had seen did not adequately cover the important areas of work – the value proposition. Also, appraisals did not happen frequently enough and, when they did take place, were usually traumatic for those involved.

"For many companies, the performance appraisal constitutes Performance Management. Well, I say that an effective Performance Management System will have no appraisal forms."

Tracy was taken aback by this. She knew that appraisal forms were not a silver bullet, but how else could a company track employee performance over time?

"Realistically, it is difficult to quantify an individual's performance on a form," Raj continued. "It is a good start but forms only part of the performance management process. The process consists of much more. Performance management starts before recruitment and ends at retirement or separation."

They were on the move again. This time, Raj took her to what appeared to be an empty factory. In the middle of the shop floor, a man sat making widgets. He labored at the task and soon had a basket full. In time, more people joined him, and production increased. There were now ten of them working on the task.

Eventually, production ground to a halt. The widgets were no longer of a standard size. Some were longer than others and the colors were different. After a brief conference with someone who looked like they were in charge, production started up again, and this time there was more regularity.

Tracy noticed that every time one of the workers made ten perfect widgets a bell would sound, and he or she would be presented with a token. The workers seemed to value it. Very soon everyone was working towards getting tokens. After a while, production slowed down again, more mistakes were made, and the workers were less excited about getting the tokens. In fact, they appeared to be bored with the whole process, and it no longer had an impact on their performance.

Their targets were increased and the tokens got bigger. But once they started achieving this new goal and got accustomed to receiving more tokens, productivity dropped again.

"Happens every time. The thing that motivated us in the beginning loses its hold once we achieve our targets regularly enough," Raj said.

"For employers, this is a nightmare, because it becomes increasingly difficult to maintain a motivated workforce. Additionally, in order to maintain competitiveness, the company must keep doing better with less. Managing performance can become quite complicated."

As time wore on, the workers on the shop floor continued their task with disinterest. Mistakes were still frequent, production was inconsistent, and there was a secondary market developing for unwanted tokens.

"Even when the value proposition is clear, it alone is not enough. Unless a company can continuously engage and motivate its employees, performance management will continue to be a struggle."

Tracy had seen many instances of this. She knew that many of her peers were bored at work. Not only that, but performance goals were unclear. They were hired to work, and that is what they did – not too well but not too badly either. There were days when Tracy felt this way too.

A large part of the motivation to work revolved around compensation. She had bills to pay and a social life to maintain. If she could afford not to work, she probably wouldn't. But there was some satisfaction in working with others – achieving goals, winning new clients, executing projects. Those things did have a pull factor. Tracy had to admit that she would miss the camaraderie and sense of belonging if she was not in a work setting.

"We are social creatures and we crave interaction. Once their basic needs are met, most people will strive to satisfy the higher order needs – a sense of achievement, accomplishment, new experiences," Raj explained.

Tracy understood this. Despite issues relating to pay, a big boost to work satisfaction occurred when goals were achieved and recognized.

"And this is where many companies get it wrong. They make motivation an issue of pay, when it is really an issue of respect."

There was a lot of action happening on the shop floor. Widgets were piling up in a haphazard manner. Several of the workers were having an argument. It was absolute chaos.

Then things started happening. The stools that they were sitting on were replaced with comfortable chairs. Each worker was given a bigger work area. The walls were covered in vibrant colors, and nice pictures were erected. A refreshment stand was placed in a corner, and a big spacious kitchen was built.

The behavior of the workers changed too. The quarreling all but disappeared and there was now laughter and collaboration. The widget count increased and so did the quality of the product.

"Do you want to improve performance? Treat employees with respect." Raj declared.

Tracy did not doubt the importance of this but she felt that there was more to it.

"It's not enough to just have nice surroundings, though. There are many volunteer groups that work in appalling conditions and yet their performance and motivation are high. What is responsible for this?"

Tracy was not sure that she knew the answer. But she would have to find out on her own because, looking up, she found that Raj was gone.

10 Old Problems, New Solutions

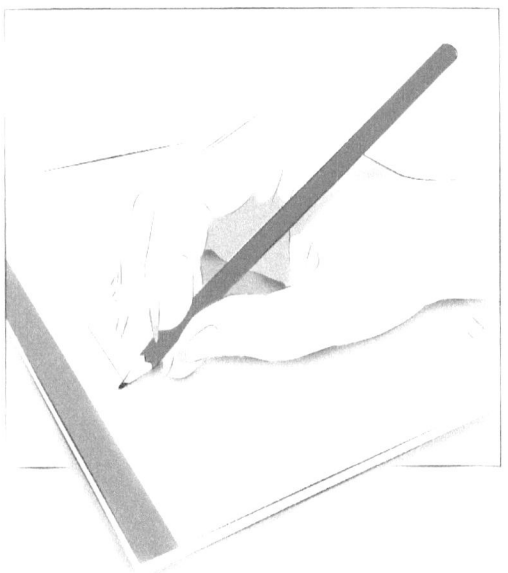

Tracy knew the drill by now. She had to come up with the next piece of the puzzle before summoning Raj again. This time, she was up to the task.

She understood that in order to measure performance, the definition of the job, and the expectation of how it should be performed had to be clear. This was the value proposition.

Now, she had to tackle the issue of motivation and how the organization could maintain the level of performance required to stay relevant and competitive.

She had always heard that money is not a motivator. At the basic level, getting paid helps everyone to maintain a certain standard of living. More money is always welcome, but it usually cannot compensate for a job that you hate or a less than favorable work environment.

In fact, she believed that it made things worse. Someone may be tempted to stay in a well paying job and continue to perform below average once the paycheck kept coming. The Performance Management System had to not only recognize when this was happening but put measures in place to prevent it.

It was unreasonable to assume that any organization could find out what motivates each individual employee and add it to the system. Some may like to start work later in the day. Some may like to leave earlier. Others may want longer vacation periods. Catering to the needs of each employee could be expensive, impractical and inefficient. Still, she was sure that there were some common threads.

She thought of the companies that ranked high in employee satisfaction globally. At some of these companies, employees dressed in a very casual manner. They brought their pets to work. There were pool tables and video games in the boardroom. She could not see that happening here. Nor did she think that it was a good idea. But she knew that those things revealed a lot about the culture of the organization. She realized something.

The extent to which a company cares about its employees shows in the way that it treats them.

No matter what the vision and mission statement says about valuing employees, actions speak louder. How much employees are valued can be seen in the quality of the restroom facilities or in the kitchen space. It shows in how workspaces are configured. A lot can be said about how much a company values its employees in its physical layout and structure.

Capital Investments Inc. did not have much of a problem in this area.

Another aspect of valuing employees relates to the way in which supervisors and managers treat employees. Where an air of mistrust dominates, productivity suffers. The 'us and them' mentality creates barriers to effective performance.

She realized that these issues influenced the culture of the organization and, as a consequence, how employees were treated and appraised.

Therefore, the next stage of the process was to get an understanding of the culture of the organization. What type of employee would succeed in this environment?

Each company has its own way of doing things which might work for some, but not for others. The management style of some managers also has an impact on how employees behave.

How was she going to identify the traits of the organization?

Tracy went through the strategic plan again, looking for clues. She wrote down the names of the persons on the management team and characterized them based on her interactions with them and what she had heard about them. She thought about others in the organization and looked for commonalities.

She was picking up certain patterns of behavior, some good and others not so great. But she was getting a clearer picture of a profile that could be used to support the Performance Management System. This profile or culture would not suit everyone, but it could help to attract candidates who value the same ideals.

As Raj had said, performance management begins before recruitment and ends at retirement or separation.

She needed to do some more research. The next day, she visited a few of the managers and asked them what some of the characteristics of effective employees were. She was not surprised that most managers described a version of themselves. But it did help her to put some things in perspective.

There is a natural bias towards seeing those that are similar to ourselves in a more favorable light.

The new Performance Management System would have to take this into account.

So far, this is what she learned:

- Defining the job is important

- There has to be a framework to recognize what motivates employees

- Respect for employees, in word and deed, is a core component

- The culture of the organization and a profile of the type of employee who would succeed as part of it must be identified

- A group of reward measures needs to be devised and should not be based on a one-size-fits-all approach

- Strategies to motivate employees have to be constantly reviewed and modified to remain relevant

- Communication of all of the above on an ongoing basis is key

She thought about feedback. It was unrealistic to get a formal review of performance once a year. Twice a year was better but still not ideal. An employee should be getting feedback every day and, in most cases, they do.

It may be a look, a smile or a frown. It's not formal, but it's feedback. It's also difficult to measure. Employees should always be able to tell how they are performing and not have to wait on a 'sit down' conversation. Those are necessary, but they should just serve to confirm what is already discussed on an ongoing basis.

This is also how, she realized, aid workers in difficult situations operate. They get immediate feedback on their work from their peers and those they care for. Sometimes this feedback comes in the form of a life saved or a life lost, but there is a direct link between what they are doing and the impact. This is not easy to replicate in organizations. Or is it?

Tracy also realized that performance management involved almost all the branches of HR. It has an impact on recruitment, compensation, training and development and succession planning. It even has an effect on office layout and design. This was a big job, but she knew where to start – with the job description.

This is how the jobs are defined. In her experience though, they were often not updated if they existed at all. She did not know of anyone who made reference to their job description on a regular basis. It usually disappeared after the start of employment with the organization and appeared again if there was some dispute about the scope of responsibility.

But the job description provides a platform for performance management, because the information contained in there can be used to define the value proposition. Not on its own though. The elements of the strategic plan, from which the departmental operational plans were drawn up, form the other key element. Departmental goals and objectives can be evaluated, and that was a key input.

She was becoming overwhelmed by the project. But before she summoned Raj again, there was something she had to do.

Tracy dug up her job description which she had not looked at since orientation week. It was a job description for a graduate trainee and was a generic document. Nothing in it spoke to what she was currently doing in any detail, and there were no guidelines or policies related to the function of a graduate trainee.

As a result, it was difficult for her to assess her own performance based on that document. She remembered her appraisal with Ms. Rogers. It was basically a review of her projects but, come to think of it, Tracy had had very little guidance or assistance in structuring the work. Much of it was left up to her discretion. Was this fair?

Yes, organizations need people who can think on their feet but context and some level of guidance was also necessary to ensure that the output was in line with what the company finds acceptable.

This could mean that, in addition to a clear job description, standard operating procedures should give more detail and context. Some of the more technical departments had them but not all.

In terms of the motivation issue, the company has to ensure that it hires persons with the passion and drive for the job from the outset. This means that:

- The job has to be clearly and accurately defined

- The recruiting process has to be able to effectively identify those who would be most successful in the role not only in terms of qualification but also attitude

This is a link that the Performance Management System has to provide, and it means that all arms of HR have to be integrated. An 'employee template' has to be created in order to select new hires and assess current ones. This template could form part of both the interviewing process as well as the appraisal process. In this way, a continuous link will be maintained throughout the work lifespan of the employee.

As the employee works their way through the organization, this template will chart their movement and can be updated as necessary. This will allow for the integration of succession planning initiatives as well as lateral moves and job enrichment opportunities. Gaps in performance can be addressed by measures such as training, coaching and mentoring. In cases where this does not work, the Performance Management System will need to allow for the redeployment or separation of the employee from the company.

Tracy could see it all coming together in her head. Now she was ready for Raj's final input.

11 The Third Question

The briefcase started attracting attention once more. Over the past couple of days, it seemed to have undergone a makeover. It looked almost like new again. Tracy started telling people that it was a different briefcase.

As she progressed along her path towards completing the project, the bag improved. She realized that it had become her performance indicator.

As I improve my output, it rewards me by looking better and getting me compliments.

She chuckled.

If only it were so easy with a Performance Management System.

In a way, she found it motivating. She had a tangible way of gauging her performance. Was there a way to get such immediate feedback on performance without the use of magic?

She still was not able to come up with a clear explanation in her head for what was happening and why but she was learning a lot and the experience was invaluable. Maybe it was just a long complicated dream. She hoped that she would get the project finished before she woke up.

Nevertheless, she felt that she was on to something with this train of thought, and her next question became clearer.

She was even talking to Rodney again. He was helping her with some aspects of the research since he was working on a compensation project. She needed to understand how the current compensation structure tied in to performance.

"Well, it doesn't really. In theory, employees who get higher performance appraisal ratings are supposed to get higher increases whenever there is profit sharing," he had told her. "But because the system is so subjective, employees with the biggest mouths tend to stand out."

It was the same with bonuses.

She had asked about other forms of compensation. He had told her that there was nothing other than financial rewards unless she wanted to count things like educational assistance and sponsored training. Even then, access to rewards was subject to bias. Some employees had negotiated special arrangements with regard to working hours, and a few persons were allowed to telecommute but she was not sure how this related to performance management.

She also spoke to one of the trainees assigned to training and development. Because of the technical nature of the work that the company did, there was a comprehensive training plan in relation to its products. There were many checks and balances, because it was not a cheap investment. There was also a Management Development Program which identified so called 'high flyers', but this only catered to those involved in the core business of the company. The Program was only specific to the income generating units.

On the whole, HR was a disjointed function. Tracy really needed some clarity quickly since her deadline for resubmission was looming.

When she had a chance to be alone in the storeroom, she quickly summoned Raj.

"Well, at the rate you are going, I did not think you would need me anymore," Raj joked, as he shook off some dust from his jacket.

"I took some time to do some cleaning, as I know I'll be moving on soon." he shared.

Tracy was sad to hear this but she knew that her time with him was coming to at an end. She shared the thoughts which she had been mulling over the last couple of days with him, and he seemed pleased.

"It certainly sounds like you're on the right track," he said.

Tracy understood the need for a clear get of goals, a well defined job description and policies and procedures, but how do you measure the measurement?

"How do you actually track performance?"

"Good question, except you can't measure it," Raj said coolly.

Tracy was getting annoyed. Why was she going through all this if performance could not be measured?

"Strictly speaking, performance is not a unit of measure. It is not finite, and it never ends. Even as people come and go, the organization still performs. What we must really be talking about is monitoring input and measuring outcomes."

Tracy still wasn't clear on what he meant.

"How do you assess a person's performance when they are not solely responsible for the output? How do you assess their contribution as a part of the whole?"

She didn't know.

"What we are really looking at is effort and output. If you want to call it performance to make things easier, fine. But that won't make it any easier to measure." Raj explained.

They were back at the widget factory where production was humming along.

It was a well integrated business now with departments, a warehouse and corporate headquarters. The original widget makers had all been promoted to heads of various departments from accounting to operations. The widget making process was now automated, and there was little human involvement. The company seemed to be doing well.

"So, who do we appraise – the robots or the applications?" Raj asked.

"Even if production was done in a more traditional way, how does one measure the performance of each employee? By the amount of widgets made? By the quality? How about the number of reworks? What about collaboration with others? What about their experience in widget-making? I can go on and on. What do you want to measure, and what will you call good performance?"

As simple as this job was, there were so many different components that could be measured.

"What we should measure is the output of widgets in terms of amount and quality," Tracy suggested, although she wasn't sure.

"Good start," Raj said. "How does that take into account the input, the level of experience and expertise in widget-making?"

Tracy had to think about that.

"That is what people get paid for – their expertise – and experience is developed on the job. This is part of the process as well," she argued, "and I guess if it's not important to the process, people don't feel a sense of pride in their ability?"

Tracy felt cornered. Part of the motivation and drive with regard to work did include one's feeling of competence. She believed though that those issues could be covered by seniority recognition, promotion and job enrichment opportunities.

"Ah, I like the way you are thinking," Raj said, reading her thoughts.

"So, do you realize that performance management is all encompassing and involves every facet of the HR function?"

Tracy had to agree. Performance management could not be isolated from other aspects of HR in the same way that an employee's performance could not be isolated from the expertise and competence that they develop on the job. This expertise and competence created value as time went on, and the company has to harness it as it is the source of competitive advantage. It was the difference between the success of one company and the failure of another.

"So, what we are talking about is the development of a work life cycle plan for each employee that takes into account all aspects of their organizational life from entry to exit." Raj continued.

This, he went on to add, had to be managed by the HR Department with significant input from line managers and supervisors.

"In the end, there is no performance management, only HR."

In that case, it wasn't a Performance Management System that she needed to create but a HR Development Plan.

But how?

"You will need to think in terms of a life cycle and factor all the elements of HR into it. I know that this should be our last consult, but I am willing to review your plan when it is done."

With that, Raj was gone.

12 The Plan

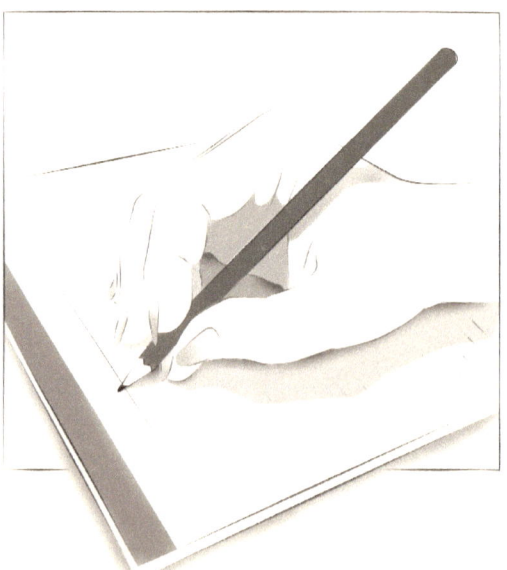

It was now the moment of truth. Tracy had to put together the plan based on all of the elements that she had learned in the last few days. Everything was still not perfectly clear, but she was sure that the process of getting it documented would help things make sense.

Here is what she came up with.

1) The Value Proposition

The first element was to create a mechanism to accurately define each job in the organization and to link it to the strategic direction of the company. The key inputs would be:

- The Strategic Plan

- The Operational Plan

- Job Descriptions

The first two were easy since they already existed. The main idea was to ensure that the elements of the strategic plan were broken down into departmental goals and objectives with milestones. This would be contained in the operational plan.

The next element was to ensure that each department had the requisite skills to meet the targets. There may be required jobs that don't exist (recruitment may be necessary), and current jobs would have to be analyzed to ensure that they were correct and in alignment with the milestones and tasks required.

This would require a **Job Analysis** exercise. Each department would need to go through an audit process of all the jobs to ensure that they reflected what the employees actually did and that they were in alignment with the tasks and requirements outlined in the strategic plan and developed in the operational plan. If necessary, new jobs could be created and this would involve the recruitment process.

As part of this process, competencies for each position would have to be generated describing the things that employees must possess in the right amount in order to be successful at their jobs. The question that must always be asked is what will a successful employee in this role be like? In other words, how will they act? How will they approach their tasks? One has to keep asking these questions.

Additionally, the updated job descriptions would be used to identify the main processes in the department, and **Standard Operating Procedures (SOPs)** would be developed. In this way, all employees, current and new, would have a clear sense of not only what is required of them but also how to get it done. This will make the process of assessing their performance simpler.

This process will have to be reviewed periodically to maintain its accuracy.

2) Culture and Motivation

The next step involves defining the culture of the organization and identifying the type of employee who would be successful in such an environment. This would be a little harder to accomplish. There were some companies that offered something called a **Culture**

Audit where, through a series of questionnaires and interviews, they are able to identify key elements of a company's culture and create a psychometric profile of the type of employee who would excel there.

Tracy knew that certain types of jobs, as well as organizations, attracted a particular personality type. This could either help or hurt. If an organization has an abundance of the same personality type, it could lead to **group think** and a lack of innovation. There is such a thing as too much consensus. On the other hand, having too many different personality types could lead to discord and high employee turnover. It is difficult to find a balance, but it helps to know where the organization stands in terms of culture.

She had neither the time nor the budget to do a formal Culture Audit, but she did have the psychometric reports of all the new hires for the last three years. An analysis of these would give a good idea of what she was looking for and with a few more assessments of the current staff she could get a representative sample to work with.

In addition, she would interview key members of the management team to get their input.

Tracy knew that she would also have to do an audit of the staff in terms of demographics, experience and interests. She was hoping that this information would help her to identify issues relating to motivation so that trends could be identified and added to the reward structure. If several members of staff were interested in fitness, the company could offer to subsidize gym fees. If there were many new parents, support could be provided to start a crèche. These initiatives would be geared towards making the company a more attractive place to work. This helps to attract talent and encourages top performers to stay.

In order to identify the skill set and level of experience of employees, she would use the **Talent Metre**[1] which she recently came across in a management book. It offered a simple way to categorize employees based on factors such as seniority, experience and contribution.

As part of the process, she would also have to look at office layout and design issues. There may be things that could be done to make the workspace more conducive to effective and efficient work. She would need to work with the Administrative Department on this project.

3) Measurement and Tracking

This was by far the most challenging aspect of the system. Once the value proposition was in place and there were departmental objectives, the objectives had to be further divided by job type for each employee.

---

[1] Reference to the Talent Metre is from the book 'Adventures of an HR Manager' by the same author.

For example, the custodians are responsible for the cleanliness and general upkeep of the offices. If they do not do this properly, it makes the day to day work in the various departments more difficult and could affect the ability of employees to meet their objectives.

The Standard Operating Procedures document should outline a process for the cleaning of different areas (washrooms versus the lobby) as well as describe the different types of cleaning methods (dusting versus mopping).

The supervisor, in collaboration with the staff, then has to set cleanliness **standards** for each area under their control. This will include a schedule indicating the number of times a particular area should be cleaned, how it should be cleaned and when to reduce disruption. It should also specify what clean looks (and smells) like. Employee names and assignments would be listed on the schedule so that they know where they should be, when they should be there and what they should be doing. This will aid in assessing performance.

For more complicated jobs, the procedures would require more effort, but she had a plan for the development of these as well.

She thought about a job like her own in which the output was more intangible and would be realized over a period. At any point in time she is working on several projects, each with different objectives, time lines and stakeholders. However, these projects should be aligned to the overall objective, or value proposition, for which her post was created and should be reflected in her job description.

Each project should have clear objectives and milestones which could be documented as part of the appraisal system and monitored by a supervisor or manager. More importantly, she should be liaising with the said manager or supervisor on the projects to get guidance and feedback. This would form part of an informal feedback loop. A more formal feedback loop could be created through the 'sit down' type evaluations that occur as part of an appraisal process.

The higher up in the organization one moves, the less specific the goals become. This brings its own challenges, but it was not an impossible scenario. For now, she had to deliver a tangible Performance Management System, and her performance would be based on this.

What about the issue of bias?

Tracy was aware that, in many cases, a manager's attitude – positive or negative – has an impact on the employee being assessed. This usually worked to the employee's disadvantage. She felt that this was caused by three main things:

1) Unclear objectives which leave ample room for interpretation

2) The lack of an audit system to allow for performance to be independently verified

3) The absence of proper coaching and forums to deal with conflict

It was important for the organization to properly define and document objectives at all levels. This requires some practice. It may also be a good idea to have a 360 degree element in some appraisals to allow other stakeholders to weigh in on an employee's performance. If this is not possible, HR will have to fulfill an audit function by looking at trends and recording feedback from employees on the appraisal process. HR must also ensure that conflict within and between departments are dealt with in a proactive manner.

She also thought of the **Primacy-Recency Effect** which describes the tendency of people to only remember the first and last events of an episode while the middle gets muddled. This could also have a negative impact on an appraisal. The tracking system would need to take this into account.

Even though Raj was not physically there, Tracy felt as though he was guiding her thought process. This is why she pulled the briefcase even closer as she started tackling what she considered to be the most difficult part of the project – the performance tracker.

13 Tracking Performance

Tracy knew that the appraisal was one of the most unpopular aspects of performance management. Managers and supervisors never liked the process, and employees usually suffered through it.

There were many reasons for this – it had no bearing on actual performance, built-in bias made it very subjective and some managers used it as a weapon to punish certain employees. The list could go on.

In her mind, the main reason was the fact that the appraisal was not linked to a value proposition, and the resultant reward structure was either used in an arbitrary manner or did not meet the needs of the population it was designed for.

She had seen some very intimidating appraisal forms. Many had terms that were open to several different interpretations.

Shortly after her first encounter with Raj, Tracy started doing most of her work in the storeroom even during the day. It soon became known as 'Tracy's Office.' She did not mind – the room was perfect because of its solitude and had a large table in the centre where she could spread out her research. Several of the graduate trainees, including Rodney, worked with her in there sometimes as she tried to piece together the project. She now had one more day left before the deadline.

The fact that sleep had been minimal did not bother her. She was more upset about missing gym time. Abdominal muscles don't make themselves. But Tracy had to admit that she was enjoying working on this project and once she was over this last hurdle she would have time for herself again.

That afternoon, she found herself in her office again. She was piecing together the final elements of the Performance Management System and was stuck on the measurement. Tracy knew that she could no longer summon Raj as all three consulting wishes had been used. He did say that he would still help her, but she had no idea how. At that moment, the answer came.

She was sitting at the table with the briefcase next to her. She was reviewing some appraisal forms she had found on the Internet when they suddenly slipped off the table. She bent to pick them up and as she did, a single sheet of paper slid to the floor.

She picked up the piece of paper. At first it seemed blank but as she focused on it, words appeared.

You can only measure what you can see.

This made sense. When it came to managing performance, the focus needed to be on observable behavior, not on interpretation or perception.

Tell them what good behavior looks like.

Another valid point. Many companies had their appraisal system set up like a test with a greater focus on failing employees. The last line appeared.

Make it simple, make it fun.

That sounded a lot simpler on paper.

She came up with the following.

The appraisal had three parts:

1) Organizational Objectives and Job Performance

2) Behavioral Skills

3) Learning and Growth

1) Organizational Objectives and Job Performance

This section was purely the value proposition. It consisted of the departmental objectives that were further subdivided into tasks and assigned to each employee within the department. The assignment of these tasks was linked directly to their job description. For the most part, these objectives were related to the day to day operations of the departments and the roles that each employee played. Tracy believed that it was important to get the core jobs right and that they should be represented in the Performance Management System. Another set of objectives were linked to stretch targets for that particular year which were cascaded down from the strategic plan and the operational plan.

For example, the ABC Company sells tires. As part of their strategic plan, they intend to become the number one brand in the country within the next five years. In order to do so, they have to improve the quality and reliability of their product. Therefore, the objective of the Procurement Department is to source high quality, cost efficient raw material for the Production Department to use.

Within the Procurement Department there are **Procurement Specialists** (employees who source material) and **Product Specialists** (employees who perform tests on material to ensure that quality standards are met).

For the Procurement Specialists, their objective and, by extension, their job is to develop a mechanism to source the best material at the best price. Within the Procurement Department, this division will develop a plan to achieve this, and each person in that position would have a specific task in order to achieve this. This plan will be documented, and projects will be assigned to specific individuals.

These objectives and tasks would form part of the appraisal system. The Procurement Specialists may have other secondary functions which may, or may not, form part of the appraisal process. This is up to the department. A similar process will be conducted for the Product Specialists.

Tracy felt that this section of the appraisal process should carry the most weight since it relates to achieving the overall target or score and concerns the core work done by the department.

2) Behavioral Skills

Another key component Tracy looked at was company culture. This refers to not only what a company does but how. This area would cover issues such as how customers should be treated, the impact of the company on the social and physical environment and the attitudes that best reflect the company's vision and mission.

This was where the research on company culture became important. The company must be able to define the 'ideal employee', from a behavioral standpoint. The kinds of behaviors that are expected, and those that are not, must be known. Part of this will be contained in the vision and mission, but it is actually manifested in how employees interact with customers and coworkers.

Having examined its culture, the company must then identify a list of traits or competencies that it would like to promote, support, and reward.

Having studied her own company's strategic plan in some detail and engaged in conversations with key stakeholders, Tracy was able to identify some traits or competencies that were valued by Capital Investments Inc.

- Leadership

- Innovation

- Strategic Thinking

- Problem Solving

- Communication Skills

She was sure that there could be more. Her premise was that both current and prospective employees should have these competencies in order to be successful at the company. But how are these employees identified?

She tackled this from two angles. Firstly, these competencies had to be properly defined. Even though there were generic definitions for all of these terms that could be found in textbooks and on the Internet, Tracy decided that it was important to have company specific definitions which reflected its particular environment.

For instance, Leadership at Capital Investments Inc. could be defined as, *'taking charge and responsibility for the sale. I own the deal. I own the result.'*

This would work nicely for the sales team and, with a little tweaking, could work for the rest of the organization as well. It does not end there. Once the competency is defined, it is necessary to identify a number of observable behaviors that could be used as proof that the particular competency was being displayed or that a person had achieved proficiency in it.

For example, the observable behaviors for Leadership could be:

- Takes charge of the client interaction by providing practical advice backed up by relevant data

- Proactively seeks out new clients and business opportunities

- Ensures that coworkers and relevant departments have the necessary information and guidance to support the sale

These definitions could be modified depending on the department. For the HR Department, an observable behavior for Leadership could be *'proactively finds solutions to areas of conflicts between departments and/or individuals.'* For innovation, *'develops and/or improves at least one key process during the period under review'* could work.

The assessed employee must be able to provide evidence, and this should be supported by the observations of the manager or supervisor. So, for the period under review, each employee should get a score that reflects his or her achievement in a particular competency.

It is likely that not all competencies will be measured in all departments and that the definitions or behavioral indicators will vary across the organization. HR has a key role in this process and in keeping it simple, Tracy realized.

Also, these traits can be assessed using psychometric testing. This is especially relevant for new hires during the recruitment phase but can also be used for current employees. Current employees, at certain levels, could be assessed once every two years or so as part of an internal Management Development Program.

3) Learning and Growth

Now that the first two areas were defined, Tracy moved on to the final section. The question before her was what to do with the data collected? By following the process, employees would have been assessed on a) their ability to perform their job and reach objectives and b) the ways in which they cultivate the right workplace attitudes. This information could then be used as a basis for training and development.

Tracy created a metric which stated that employees who achieved a certain score in the outlined areas would be eligible for specific types of training interventions.

For example,

- Employees with high scores could be enrolled in an accelerated management program which could lead to promotion and secondment. They could also become coaches or mentors to other employees and be eligible for the highest level of rewards which could be a mix of monetary and nonmonetary.

- Employees with 'middle of the road' scores could receive specific training, be assigned a mentor or coach from within the organization and be eligible for a basic level of rewards.

- Employees with 'below average' scores could go through a second period of assessment, similar to probation, during which they can also be exposed to targeted training and mentoring. They would need to be assessed more frequently and a lack of improvement could mean a transfer, lack of promotion opportunities or eventual separation if there is no improvement over time.

In this way, all employees, regardless of their performance levels, would be exposed to some form of training and development. Naturally, their performance in these initiatives would also be assessed and scored as part of their evaluation.

In the end, Tracy felt confident that she had covered all the bases. All that was left to do was to present this to Ms. Rogers.

14 In The End

Tracy was able to meet her deadline. By the time she had to do her presentation, the briefcase was shiny and new – a reflection of her new disposition. The last week had been unforgettable. She was still not entirely convinced that the events were not part of some elaborate dream, but the project was completed and that was all that mattered right now. She had her presentation to do for Ms. Rogers, and for the first time she was looking forward to it.

As usual, she was on time. Tracy went through all of her findings and presented her plan with great attention to detail. Ms. Rogers said nothing but took copious notes. Tracy knew that the questions would be many and difficult.

After about an hour, Tracy wrapped up the presentation. She felt very light as though a massive burden had been taken off her shoulders. Without a pause, the questions began.

How would she get information for the Value Proposition?

Tracy felt that, notwithstanding the fact that the HR Director was part of the team that developed the company's strategic plan, HR would have a key role in dissecting it in order to identify the objectives for each department and each job. To do this, HR would have to work closely with the Head of each department in the development and documentation of their operational plans. It made more sense to work with them rather than wait until it was presented. This way, all the necessary clarification of definitions can be made. Additionally, HR would be able to give direct input in terms of the impact the plan could have on staffing, training and performance management itself.

When the operational plans were completed, HR would have all of the outputs needed to update the performance appraisal system for the next financial year.

Tracy believed that it was important for the employees to know at the beginning of the period what they were being evaluated on, because the premise was that the company wanted everyone to pass and not be surprised or confronted during their appraisal with objectives that they may not have fully been aware of.

Once the new objectives were added, there would be a period during which it would be circulated to staff for clarification and sign-off. Of course, HR would play a key role in coordinating this process.

Tracy proposed that there be two periods of evaluation each year – a mid-year review and a final review to coincide with the end of the financial year. Managers and supervisors would also have the option of giving monthly updates on performance so that they would not have to go through the entire process in one sitting. She also proposed that employees could flag performance issues at any time during the period of review which would help to improve the process.

Tracy had verified that there was no need to implement an expensive Human Resource Information System (HRIS) to do this. In the interim, spreadsheets and reports would work, plus it was always better to work out the format for the system before purchasing any software so that it could be put to the best use when installed.

How do we account for different types of employees?

It would be impractical to have the same type of appraisal for the Finance Manager and the Chief Custodian. However, the principles remained the same. Each appraisal will have the same components.

- Departmental Objectives (value proposition)

- Company Culture and Attitude (behavioral competencies)

- Leaning and Growth (training and development)

The appraisal format will differ by department and even by employee, since it will be based primarily on job function. Additionally, the behavioral competencies may also vary according to department. For example, competencies that are related to sales and marketing ability will be important to the Sales Department but not to the Records Department. Apart from overall competencies that will be identified for the entire company, each department will also identify those that are specific to their operations.

This process of competency identification was another important aspect of the system. HR will have to undertake a Culture Audit, or a similar type of intervention, in order to identify and define the key competencies required for the company to succeed. This would be done on a company-wide and departmental level and would be reviewed every three to five years to ensure relevance.

After the competencies are identified, the HR Department would incorporate them into the appraisal system and employees would be assessed against the standard.

How would the training and development plan work?

All training done by the company will be informed by the structure of the Performance Management System. A key component would be the identification of training needs. In some cases, training would be necessary for continuous improvement in order to build on and/or improve competencies in a particular area (new or pre-existing). For instance, if the company was developing new financial products it may become necessary for some members of staff to be exposed to certain types of training so that this learning can be employed internally.

Alternatively, training may be required where gaps in performance have been identified through the Performance Management System. As part of the appraisal process, supervisors or managers will identify gaps in performance that can be addressed with training, coaching or mentoring and will coordinate these activities with HR. The HR Department will be responsible for scheduling and budgeting and will work with the departments to ensure that the intervention is evaluated and knowledge transfer occurs. Employees would also be assessed on this.

In time, the HR Department will be better able to forecast training needs and ensure better budgeting.

In both cases, the framework allows for training and development to be assessed and reported on as part of the employee's overall performance.

Many times, employees attend training and very little transfer of knowledge occurs. Linking it to performance helps in measurement and ensures that the employee implements what he or she has learned so that their overall performance score can be higher.

What about the Rewards and Recognition?

This also has several levels depending on factors such as seniority, department and compensation level. There would be two main types of rewards – monetary and non-monetary.

- Monetary – As the name suggests, this will include pay increases, bonuses, shares and deferred compensation schemes.

- Non-monetary – This will include things such as flexible hours, telecommuting, departmental and company awards and a few other innovative ideas that staff members came up with.

Based on score and ranking, employees will be eligible for certain types of rewards. Different categories of employees would have access to different rewards.

Tracy added that it was imperative that the company provide a safe and functional environment for employees since performance at work can be negatively affected by issues such as a lack of resources and a cluttered or unsafe work environment. As such, HR would work with the Facilities Department to ensure that, as far as possible and within budget limits, these issues are addressed.

She also felt that the some benefits should not be linked directly to performance but should reflect the values of the company. For instance, she knew that health and wellness were important to the CEO who was an avid runner and cyclist. Initiatives such as gym membership, company participation in races and sporting events and even sponsorship of such events could be done in order to encourage staff participation and reward those who participate on an ongoing basis.

Tracy suggested that an events committee, made up of employees from across the organization, should be set up to handle such events and programs as a way of supporting these initiatives. She had always liked the idea of a crèche or day care service for parents with young children and company-sponsored breakfast a few times per month. The committee could look at the feasibility of such programs.

It was important to let employees know that they are valued, and these activities could help in this regard.

How would appraisals be scored?

This area could be complicated, but it was essential to the success of the program. Tracy believed that the weighting of the three areas under review would have to be different. All areas were important but some had a greater impact on the bottom line.

She believed that a 50/30/20 rule could be applied.

- 50% for Organizational Effectiveness and Job Performance

- 30% for Behavioral Skills

- 20% for Learning and Growth

Organizational Effectiveness and Job Performance had the greatest impact on the company's performance, thus the higher rating. It was also the area that contained the most objective measurements. Either the employee met his or her objectives or not, and there could be a scale to determine the extent of the achievement.

The Behavioral component was more subjective. Tracy proposed the development of a guide which would identify a list of **observable behavior** to support these competencies. For example, the objective evidence for Teamwork could be *'works well with others, involves coworkers in getting the task done and usually volunteers for team activities.'* Similarly, each competency would have a shortlist of examples to guide the supervisor or manager in assessing the employee.

In terms of Learning and Growth, employees would not only be assessed on the training they complete but also on their ability to transfer the knowledge within their department and contribute to the cross training of their peers. Tracy believed that at least two persons should be competent in each job within a department, where possible, to ensure coverage if one person is absent.

Naturally, the scale could be adjusted depending on where the organization wants to place a greater focus. If workplace culture and attitude is an issue, a higher weighting can be placed on this area. The same applies if there is a drive to promote learning and knowledge transfer.

What is the implementation plan?

Tracy had spent a considerable amount of time on this aspect of the project. She had started some of the work already but in order for it to be ready for company-wide implementation, much more needed to be done. There were several phases to the implementation.

- Research

- Design

- Pilot/Rollout

Research

Some was done already, but a comprehensive data gathering phase was required. This needed to include the following:

- Analysis of past and present strategic plans to identify trends in performance objectives and company values

- Interviews with key staff members to identify key aspects of company culture

- Psychometric assessments of a representative group of employees to determine the range of competencies present in the company

- Survey of employees to identify types of rewards and recognition preferences

- Survey of key clients to ascertain strengths and areas for improvement as it relates to service delivery

This information would be used to:

- Identify key aspects of the company's culture which will be used to develop the behavioral skills component

- Identify the types of reward and recognition structures that are preferred so that their feasibility can be determined

- Assist in the determination of the value proposition.

This process could take three to six months depending on the level of detail required and the number of HR personnel assigned to the project.

Design

Once the research phase was completed, the data would be used to design the Performance Management System. This would include:

- The review and updating of job descriptions

- Documentation of departmental and individual objectives

- The creation of job bands with corresponding rewards

- Definitions of behavioral competencies

- Development of a training plan

- Design of a performance appraisal form

Tracy had already designed a draft of some of these items based on the work that she had already done. Additionally, some areas could be completed before all of the research was completed. However, the completion of the appraisal form was essential to the progress of the process and could only be constructed when all of the research elements were completed.

She expected to have this done within a month of the final research findings.

Key to this phase is the submission of an interim budget which is essential in determining the extent to which the company can afford to implement the system. Planning the exercise in this way makes it a bit easier to forecast the cost and various scenarios could be run in order to determine this. Key costs would include rewards, both financial and non-financial, as well as training.

Some cost savings are expected with the new streamlined system and areas such as recruitment and succession planning will get a boost as well. In particular, the recruitment procedure would be redesigned to match the appraisal format. In this way, prospective employees would be assessed in a similar fashion to current employees in terms of job knowledge and behavioral competencies.

Ms. Rogers seemed satisfied with her responses. It was difficult to tell because her facial expression hardly changed during the presentation or the question and answer session.

Tracy was actually surprised that there were so few questions but she was not unduly worried. She felt that she had done her best even if Ms. Rogers was not satisfied. The last couple of weeks had been quite an experience, and she needed time for it all to soak in.

She had not seen Raj since their last encounter and was unsure of what was supposed to happen next. Did she have to keep the briefcase? Should she put it back? She did not know that the answer would soon come from the most unlikely of sources.

"Tracy, you did an excellent job," Ms. Rogers said with a broad smile. "You covered all the bases and exceeded my expectations."

As Tracy tried to come to terms with the praise that just came from a person who seldom smiled or gave praise, she was handed a bigger surprise.

"I see that our mutual friend has not lost his touch," Ms. Rogers chuckled as if it were a private joke. "Oh, and he said that you should put the bag back in case someone else needs help in the future."

Epilogue

Eight months have passed since the presentation and things are coming along well. Tracy is one of the few graduates kept on by Capital Investments Inc. and she now holds the post of Senior HR Officer. She has the most senior position among all the graduates.

Rodney was still here as well, and they were both coordinating the Performance Management System project. It had been a lot of work. They were able to finish the research phase within four months but not without challenges. Some of the senior executives voiced their disapproval of junior employees working on such a significant project with confidential aspects, but Ms Rogers surprised her again by strongly backing their work and shooting down the objections. Their relationship had improved dramatically as well and Tracy now reported directly to her.

They did not speak about Raj, but Tracy realized soon after the presentation that he must have helped Ms. Rogers in a similar way in the past. She had no idea how long ago that might have been and did not want to ask. Ms. Rogers had been there for about twenty years so it could have been years ago. Following her advice, Tracy had put the briefcase back into the filing cabinet where she first found it and never went back to the storeroom. At times, she was tempted to go and look for it but had not yet given in to the temptation. In any event, she had a lot of work to do.

For parts of the research she and Rodney had to travel to some of the subsidiaries, and this made them the envy of the other graduates.

They had just completed the design phase which took a bit longer than planned. On a whole it balanced out because the research phase was completed ahead of schedule.

Piloting was recently started in the Records Department. She had worked closely with Mr. Gregg on his departmental objectives and the format they had worked out was replicated in the other departments. It was difficult going through the process the first time, but she knew that it would be easier going forward.

The new appraisal format had been finalized and was being tested by Mr. Gregg. Once tested successfully, it would be released to all the departments. So far, the feedback noted that the process was less cumbersome and much more relevant to the work that is actually done. This was the intention.

There was some controversy over the rewards and recognition component of the project. The senior executives insisted that their reward scheme be kept confidential. Ms. Rogers conceded on this point and manages this personally. Additionally, the appraisal for senior executives has a different structure from general staff and is also managed by the HR Director. Tracy had no quarrel with this. She found the executives to be a very fussy bunch.

Some of the staff also came up with very creative but outlandish rewards which could not be included. Overall, they were able to develop a good mix and shortlist an affordable range of initiatives that could be implemented.

There were a few unexpected benefits as well. The streamlining of the training plan led to significant savings in the training budget as some duplication was removed, and they were able to negotiate better prices from service providers and consultants. The lives of the recruiters were also made easier as they now had a template, including questions, to use for all interviews.

Ms. Rogers had been the biggest revelation for Tracy. She realized that the HR Director had a very prominent role within the company and was a valued member of the senior executive team. Past the abrasive exterior, she was actually a very kind and supportive person. This did not mean that she would accept mediocre work. There were several times when she challenged Tracy to do better and to try different things. It worked out in the end.

Tracy had gotten several job offers over the past few months. The HR community was small, and word got around about the work she was doing at Capital Investments Inc. But she was determined to see the process through. In a way, she decided that the work itself was its own reward. She was highly motivated, worked longer hours when she had to, and thoroughly enjoyed working with her team members. It was not about the money – not entirely. She understood the importance of having meaningful work and it certainly made a difference in her attitude towards her work and her employer.

She realized that many people who were unhappy at work were suffering from a lack of meaning in their own work. Many of them loved what they did in terms of the actual work but detested the work environment, the physical as well as the psychosocial. Employers had a responsibility to provide not only a safe environment but a wholesome one as well.

As an HR practitioner, Tracy decided that she would dedicate her work to providing such an environment wherever her career took her. Somehow, she felt that Raj would approve.

END.

ABOUT THE AUTHOR

Jeremy Francis

Beyond Consulting (Managing Director): jeremy.francis@beyondconsultingtt.com

Areas of Interest

Focused on building the technical capacity of his clients, Jeremy founded Beyond Consulting in 2009 to provide best-in-class training and consultancy in Assessment/Development Centres and Psychometrics in the Caribbean. His main focus is using international benchmarks when providing training and services in the areas of Assessment/Development Centres, Psychometric Assessments, Coaching and General HR consulting.

Work History:

Managing Director, Beyond Consulting (2009-present)

Qualifications and Memberships

Jeremy currently holds a B.Sc in Psychology with Sociology (University of the West Indies- UWI, 2000) and a Post Graduate Diploma, in Human Resource Management (UWI, 2003). He is trained in Psychometric Test Administration and Feedback- Level A & B, British Psychological Society (BPS, Saville Wave, 2008). He is also certified as an Assessment/Development Centre Assessor (a&dc, ILM, 2009), in Assessment/Development Centre Design and Management (a&dc, ILM, 2009) and has a certificate in Coaching (Centre for Coaching, ILM 2013). He is trained to deliver the a&dc Core and Advanced Assessor Skills Course (a&dc, 2016); is a Graduate Member of the British Psychological Society (BPS), and a Member (Practitioner) of the Association for Business Psychology (ABP).

Assessment Experience

Assessment for Recruitment and Development: Proficient in the use of psychometric assessments for Recruitment/Selection, Management Development and Coaching. This has included the design and development of Personal Development Plans (PDP's) for clients. He has also designed and managed many Assessment Centres (Centre Manager and Assessor) from 2010 to the present. Additionally, Jeremy has arranged the training and certification of local HR practitioners as Assessment Centre Assessors.

HR Consulting: Designed and developed Performance Management Systems for several clients, as well as providing general HR consultancy support to small and mid-sized businesses.

Training: Co-facilitated several training courses including Assessor Skills and Saville Wave Transfer. Developed various workshops in areas related to HR and Process Management.

Other Interests

Jeremy was the Public Relations Officer of the Trinidad & Tobago Triathlon Association (TTTF) from 2013/15, and has been involved with the St. Vincent De Paul Society (SVP) in his Parish of St. Ann's for the past 4 years. He is also an avid runner and cyclist, and has participated in over 30 road and trail races locally and abroad over the past 5 years- including completing the UWI Half Marathon on 5 occasions.

He is also an avid blogger on all things Management and HR, and has compiled over 130 articles on the subject over the past two years. He is frequently contacted by HR professionals both locally and abroad on his articles, which are usually posted on the business networking site LinkedIn.

Other books by the Author:

Available on Amazon (paperback and Kindle).

The 5-Dollar Performance Management System.

From LinkedIn, By Jeremy Francis

Recently, my wife decided to reward one of our kids with five dollars, for 'listening and following instructions.' She aimed to celebrate the good behaviour, but also to let the other two see the benefits of listening to mommy and daddy. And while the eldest was over the moon, her brother and sister threw some serious shade her way.

'I don't want five dollars anyway', was one comment. After that, she was teased, until I had to step in and make threats (and remind them of the times they got rewards too).

Kids will be kids. Until I realised that when it comes to Performance Management, adults behave in much the same way.

Have you ever gotten a reward or bonus for being a 'star performer?' Or got a bigger bonus (or promotion) because of above average performance? Were your co-workers happy for you? To save face, there would have been outward signs of congratulations.

But you know what's really going on in their minds.

And if it happened to someone else, were you happy for them, or do we usually feel like we deserved it too?

And that dear friend, is the problem with most Performance Management Systems- they tend to do more to de-motivate employees than motivate them- when administered improperly.

And more often than not, they are administered improperly. If your Performance Management System is based solely on filling out an appraisal form once or twice a year, you are doing it wrong. If it is based solely on monetary rewards, you are also doing it wrong.

Our daughter would have been quite happy with just verbal praise and public affirmation for her behaviour. However, the cash changed everything, at least for the others. It raised the game. Because in our society, money stands for more than the ability to pay the bills. It is a status symbol- it is a prize. And this is installed at a young age.

Once you pay out, a mere 'congratulations' won't work anymore- you have to keep doing it.

Hey, I got no issues with money. In fact, I'm quite fond of it. But I just realised that when cash is involved in incentive programs, the details have to be clear.

So for instance, if the other kids had known that cash was on offer, they may have complied with mommy's request, without having to be asked twice. In the same way- if employees know what they have to do to get the bonus, chances are they will get it done so that they can receive it. But is this the kind of behaviour that you want to reward?

A bonus or reward should be given for instances where kids- or employees go above and beyond- when they act selflessly for the benefits of others (or the organisation)- not because they will get five dollars for their effort.

The reward for my daughter was great because she did not expect to get it. It wasn't great for her siblings because if had they known it was on offer, they might have 'behaved' too. And that defeats the purpose of rewards systems.

Most of our rewards systems treat humans like a hamster in a cage, or a monkey in a clinical trial- response (positive) equals reward. However, response (negative) usually equals... nothing. Not even feedback.

But human behaviour is so much more than that.

So how do we devise Performance Management Systems for humans?

Firstly they have to be based on feedback. People need to be told on a regular basis what they are doing right (and wrong). For that to happen, they need to be clear on what they have to do (Job descriptions, specifications etc.). They have to be qualified and capable (good job fit), and they must have the tools to function effectively.

Then, and only then, can we talk about rewards. And even then, you can't reward employees for doing their job. They get paid, don't they?

You should be rewarding exceptional work and work ethic. And while a monetary reward is great, first and foremost should be public recognition, outlining exactly what they did, the impact it had, and how it made you (and the customer) feel. I can almost guarantee you that that will go a longer way than a temporary bump in the pay-check (though that helps too).

Employees do deserve to have they pay reviewed and adjusted. And poor performers should not receive the same benefit as the others.

But then again, you shouldn't be paying poor performers anyway- you should be firing them (after giving them ample avenues to improve their performance, of course).

And that is what a Performance Management System is supposed to do- improve job performance, not just reward the 'good ones.'

So as I continue to roll our Performance Management Systems for my clients, I will make a note to integrate this 5-dollar policy into it. Who knows, it just might work.

HR is Waste Management.

From LinkedIn, By Jeremy Francis

I think that HR as a concept is past its prime. Way past. At least the way that many organisations are doing it. Over the years, I constantly bump into people in organisations that literally beg me to get them a new job. Even people in HR.

It's so bad that I will be launching a recruitment service later this year. It also sparked my company tagline: Happy at Work, back in 2010.

A lot of organisations waste Human Resources. They take a perfectly fine human being and attempt to turn them into an automated drone. I say attempt because it fails most of the time. They usually end up with an angry, passive-aggressive horde, who take it out on their customers. This isn't always the case. But it happens enough times to be the source of major concern.

Call it Employee Engagement if you wish, but people just don't like working for your company. And you can tell. They habitually come in late. Absenteeism is a major problem. Participation in company events is at an all-time low. They just do as they're told. Sound familiar?

Want to know why this happens? It's because of Job Descriptions.

Essentially, you hire someone to do a job and then put them in a box. You underutilize them. And whenever they try to expand their range and have ideas 'outside of the box', your company and HR policies shove them right back in. In the main, many employees in many organisations are not encouraged to cross-train or get involved in areas outside their main scope of work. Even where they prove to have an ability. And when they do, it is discouraged.

I know this, because it happened to me. I started seeing business opportunities and avenues for growth in my career, and by extension, the company. As soon as I started to explore them and ask the company to assist, I ran into trouble with management. I was told to focus on my job. That's not what you were hired to do. So I quit and started my own business, and expanded those opportunities on my own (with no regrets).

I have seen so many instances of bright, innovative employees, being stifled into a job that does not recognize, or utilize their talent. Employees that could become the driving force for change and growth. Many leave. But others stay, and become toxic. Then the management complains about low productivity, and refuse to improve working conditions and pay. And the wonderful spiral continues. How to you fix this?

Recognize the talents that your employees possess. This means that you have to pay attention to them. Notice the things that they can work on for hours without stopping. And recognize the things that bore them to death.

The Accounts clerk shows an interest in Marketing? Let them explore it. Has the receptionist a knack for documentation? Let her try. In my career, I went from Operations to HR, IT, Process Improvement, Logistics then HR Consulting in nine years. And it wasn't because there was a plan- or that the companies I worked in allowed it. It was because I was bored, and forced the issue. I did stuff that others didn't want to do and made it my own. For many years, my job description made no sense, because it crossed so many organisational boundaries. And no one knew how to manage me, so I was largely left alone.

Because of that, I'm able to function quite well as a consultant, because I worked in so many different areas of the business. But like I said, it wasn't planned, and at times it was very frustrating.

Do it, but with a plan. Don't manage them by job description. Or even by Objectives. Manage them by Interest (MBI).

How to Improve the Recruitment Process.

From LinkedIn, By Jeremy Francis

In conversations with HR practitioners over the years, one of the main problems they all have in common is finding and keeping the best talent. This isn't surprising- we live in a small society and in many instances, some of the best performers are abroad, excelling in foreign jurisdictions. Of course, there is great talent on the island, but the companies that have them do their best to keep them.

However, many organisations hamper their own success in the way they go about the recruitment process. I'll give a few examples.

Company A is looking for a new Marketing Director, so naturally, we ask for a Job Description (JD). The one we received seemed to be lacking, so we asked when it was last updated. 'Er... some years ago...' Now, there is nothing wrong with this necessarily. A well-constructed JD can stand the test of time; but when you are looking at a field such as Marketing, with the growing influence of social media and search optimization, companies want to ensure that a new hire has had at least some exposure to these new trends- and the JD should reflect that.

Company B was also looking for a Marketing Director. They didn't even have a JD. Or at least what they called a JD was actually a job specification. And in both examples neither company had any clearly defined performance criteria for either of the roles.

So how do we expect the Recruitment process to run smoothly?

In both cases, we had to help the company along the path, but if you are a month behind finding the new hire, is there enough time to revise a JD? The JD is the end product- a Job Analysis has to be done, and before that, there should be some semblance of a Competency Framework- which is built from the Strategic Plan of the company. You would be surprised to know how rare it is to find all these ducks in a row in local companies.

Naturally all of this is a lot of work, and when you consider that the HR department may be under-resourced and under-funded, it is easy to understand how difficult it may be to have a 'perfect' system. Unfortunately, if the building blocks of recruitment are not in place, there will be quite a bit of 'luck and chance' in the recruitment and management development processes in a company.

This is why having a properly defined Competency Model and

accurate Job Descriptions are essential- they are the foundation of the entire HR lifecycle.

And when it comes to Assessment Centres, this is especially key.

Assessment Centres are defined as follows: *Multiple assessment process involving a number of individuals undertaking a variety of activities observed by a team of trained Assessors who evaluate performance against a set of pre-determined, job-related assessment criteria.*

Basically it is a test, where prospective hires compete for a job- not dissimilar to a Game of Thrones episode, but without the conspiracies, murder and dragons. Well not really. It more approximates a highly structured event, where participants are asked to prove their competence in a number of key job-related areas- in an objective and quantifiable manner.

The definition goes on the say that: '*The activities shall include Exercises and may also include, but not be limited to standardised tests, and structured interviews. It is likely to be used to support decision making in a selection, placement or promotion context with the Participants competing against each other.*'

Assessment Centres are one of the best ways to hire at the management and executive level. Why?

They employ a multipronged approach to selecting the best

candidate. These include:

Multiple Competencies: The candidates are assessed on a number of work-related behaviours (competencies); usually between 5-10. These competencies can include areas such as Leadership, Effective Communication, Empathy and Drive. Typically, each organisation would interpret and define these in different ways- *hence the importance of having a well-defined Competency Framework in place to inform the process.* It can be done without one, but the consultant will have to either use theirs, or assist the company in hastily putting one together from whatever information is available. Either way, it will increase the costs to the organisation.

Multiple Methods: AC's use several different ways of testing a candidate's competence. Typically AC's will consist of a mix of Analysis Exercises (AE), Interview Simulations (IS), Fact Find exercises (FF), InBox or In-Basket (IN-B), and/or Day in the Life Exercises (DLE). Any one of these exercises can be as short as 40 minutes, or as long as 3 hours. An actual AC day can be as long as 8 hours- a typical work day.

Multiple Assessors: For each candidate, there is a minimum of 2 trained assessors monitoring their performance, using a standardised framework. This way, the final discussion is judged on the opinion on many.

Multiple Participants: For there to be a winner, there has to be losers. We have participated in assessment centres with as many as 8 candidates, and as few as 2. There is little benefit to having one participant as there is no one to compare results with.

Shared Data: Once the Centre is complete, there is a process where all of the data gathered throughout the process is shared and discussed (the wash-up). At this point the final points are tabulated, and the participants are ranked by performance. Note that the AC is part of the recruitment process, **and the participant with the highest score may not necessarily be the successful candidate**. This largely depends on the influence of other data sets (like reference checks, higher weighting for internal candidates etc.).

One thing is for certain- at the end of an AC process, the organisation is guaranteed to have a clear picture of the strengths and areas of improvement of each candidate for recruitment. The AC process can also be used for the development of internal candidates (like succession planning and the identification of training), through the use of Development Centres (DC).

Having said all this, you would now recognise the importance of having a clearly defined competency framework for the organisation.

Not only does it assist in making your recruitment processes more structured and successful, but ties all of these elements (like Assessment and Development Centres) into a cohesive whole.